AF595929

The Kimberleys is at the top of Western Australia. The First Nations' People lived in many areas next to the sea. The food from the sea included seaweed, fish and shellfish. Shellfish included any seafood which was contained within a shell. One of these foods was the pearl shell. Pearls form inside the shell. These are beautiful and are wanted by many people. These special pearls are called South Seas Pearls. These pearls only grow close to Australia. First Nations' People left the pearl shells in middens on islands and the coast.

The pearl forms from a piece of sand or shell. The pearl shell covers the unwanted material in shell material. This forms a round bubble which is the pearl. The pearl grows bigger and finally, the shell gets rid of the pearl. This is similar to a skin cut or rash where it forms a scar. The pearl shell is able to form pearl material around the object to stop it hurting the pearl shell animal. This animal is called a mollusc.

Many people came to Broome searching for pearls. The first pearling people used the First Nations' People to dive for the pearls. The diver swam right down to the ocean floor to collect the pearl shells. The First Nations' People were good divers and knew the areas very well. It was hard work diving to the bottom of the sea and you had to be very strong.

Diving off Broome was very dangerous. Hammerhead sharks and other sharks lived in these warm waters. If you dived too deep you could black out. When you faint or black out, it is caused from lack of oxygen to the brain. If you are on land it is possible to wake up, but in the water, you will drown. Many First Nations' divers and other people have died while diving for pearls.

First Nations' People would dive from the boats and hold their breath for a long time. The pearl shells would be put into a bag. The bag would be taken back to the boat. The shells would be opened on the boat or on the beach. Not all the shells had a pearl. South Sea Pearls were valuable because people wanted more than could be found. The demand for them was greater than the supply.

Mother of pearl shell was used to make buttons. Old clothes still have these beautiful shell buttons. People loved pearl shell buttons. With this increased demand, more people came looking for pearls and pearl shells. Divers came from Japan and Malaya to dive for pearls and shells.

The boats were called pearl luggers. The sea off Broome was dotted with pearl luggers. The boats went up and down the coast looking for wild pearl shells and pearls. The number of shells in the sea is limited, and it takes time for the pearl shells and pearls, to grow.

Diving suits were used. This allowed more time on the sea floor. The diver had a hose connected to the pearl lugger which pumped air down into the helmet. The boat would move slowly along and the diver would walk on the sea floor. The diver looked for pearl shells. A motor would pump air to the divers via a long hose but it was still dangerous. If the hose bent or broke, the diver could drown quickly. Today, divers do not use this type of dive suit. Divers today use light weight gear and small face masks.

The boots were made of heavy lead to help the diver to sink to the ocean floor. The boots kept the diver from floating. The diver had to be very careful. If he went too deep, he could suffer from the bends. If he got stuck, it was hard to get out of the dive suit. The diver could drown before getting him back to the boat.

Broome is a different place today. It is a modern town with many First Nations' People. It has lots of other people from across the world. Some of these people had parents and grandparents who were pearlers. It is called the Gateway to the Kimberleys. There are beaches along the coast and beautiful boab trees everywhere.

Pearls are still very important for Broome. The pearls are grown in farms. The pearl shell has a fragment put inside the shell. The pearl then grows in layers around this fragment. The pearls are grown in racks in the sea. Many people work on these pearl farms. First Nations' People are still working in the pearl industry. Some of them work on the farms, and some work in shops selling pearls to tourists. The shell middens of the First People can still be found on the shores and the islands. What was once seafood for the First Peoples has now turned into a big industry. The South Seas pearls will always be wanted by people seeking beauty.

Word bank

Kimberleys	dangerous
Australia	hammerhead
pearls	oxygen
buttons	valuable
beautiful	fragment
helmet	tourists
luggers	floating
allowed	islands
dangerous	Japan
drown	Malaya
shellfish	lugger
material	midden
object	mollusc
Broome	industry